Terry Heathcote's enthusia
wildlife turned him into a
writer and lecturer in the early 1980s – since when
his photographs have appeared in innumerable
magazines, both at home and abroad. His main
interest has long been the wildlife of the New Forest,
where he lives, but his work now embraces a range of
subjects. His books include *Guide to the New Forest,
Wild Heritage* and *The New Forest, a Portrait in
Colour*, for which the late Jack Hargreaves wrote the
text.

Following page
Holidaymakers and stock
Markway, the New Forest

Photographs and Text
TERRY HEATHCOTE

———————

THE DOVECOTE PRESS

THE NEW FOREST

A Discovery Book
for Children

First published in 1998 by The Dovecote Press Ltd
Stanbridge, Wimborne, Dorset BH21 4JD

ISBN 1 874336 45 8

Typeset by the Typesetting Bureau
Printed and bound in Singapore

CONTENTS

USING THIS BOOK

The clues to the story of the Forest, how it works, the people involved and the wildlife are to be seen all around and finding them can greatly add to the enjoyment and understanding of this fascinating corner of England.

Whether on holiday, visiting for the day or living in the area, these clues can be found in every part of the Forest and of over seventy pictured and described, all but one can be found and seen throughout the year, and none of them involves any sort of entry fee.

The subjects vary in difficulty, which is indicated by stars. These range from a single star for the most easy to five stars for the most difficult. In all there are a total of 215 stars to aim for.

INTRODUCTION

It is now over nine hundred years since King William I, known as William the Conqueror, created his first royal hunting forest, calling it 'Nova Foresta' or New Forest. Then, as now, most of the area was a wilderness of old woodland, heaths and bogs with just the odd cottage and small village scattered here and there.

The whole forest was taken into the ownership of the Crown and the King introduced special laws, known as Forest Law, to protect the deer and other game for his own hunting pleasure. The punishment for breaking these laws could be very harsh and included blinding, cutting off hands and hanging. But although the people living in and around the Forest were not allowed to interfere with the deer in any way, they were allowed to do certain things which today we know as common rights. All these rights are now attached to properties and it is the people who occupy these properties, known as commoners, who are allowed to practice them.

Some commoners have the right to turn out pigs each autumn. Others have the right to gather fuelwood to burn on the fire at home, and just a few have the right to graze sheep in the Forest. But the most popular right of all is the one that allows the commoners to turn out ponies, cattle and donkeys to feed on the Forest. All of these are branded to show which commoner actually owns them.

Timber has been grown in the Forest for centuries. Originally the main need was for small timber. This involved either coppicing, cutting off the tree at ground level to encourage it to send up a mass of new shoots, or pollarding, cutting of trees at head height so the new shoots were out of reach of ponies and deer.

Gradually the need changed to bigger timber, especially oak trees to build the great wooden warships needed by the Royal Navy. About three hundred years ago this resulted in tree pollarding being made illegal and large areas of the Forest being fenced off to grow the oaks. Today, although few of the original oaks remain, the Inclosures used to grow them are still found throughout the Forest, with many now being used to grow conifers.

The old woods, heaths and bogs that make up much of the Forest are becoming increasingly unusual elsewhere in the country, and so is the wildlife. There are deer, badgers, foxes and grey squirrels, as well as a huge variety of birds, insects and flowers. Although these are not always easy to spot, there are two places where wildlife will invariably be seen. At the Bolderwood Deer Sanctuary regular afternoon feeding attracts fallow deer at most times of the year. The Reptiliary at Holidays Hill near Lyndhurst contains snakes, lizards, frogs and toads which can be seen throughout the summer.

Looking after the wildlife and managing the Forest is the work of the Forestry Commission. There are keepers who look after their own particular part of the Forest and are especially involved with the wildlife. Other staff are concerned with planting and harvesting the trees. Some ensure there is sufficient grazing by maintaining the ditches and burning off the old heather and gorse. The remainder are mainly concerned with all the visitors and such things as the caravan sites, car parks and waymarked walks.

1. ALDER CARR

Alder trees grow in wet situations, sometimes scattered along stream edges or, where the ground is boggy either side of the stream, as a line of woodland known as an alder carr. In most of these carrs nearly all the trees have many small trunks growing from the roots as a result of them being coppiced - cut off at ground level to encourage new growth. In the past these were harvested and then burnt to make a very fine charcoal which was greatly valued.

Difficulty:　★ ★ ★
Where:　Wet areas
Date seen:

2. BADGER SETT

There are a good number of badger setts scattered throughout the Forest woodlands. Some of them are very large with many entrances, some are much smaller and there are others which have either been abandoned or are only used occasionally. Many of them are on sloping ground and just inside a woodland edge. Active setts often have fresh digging at the entrances, sometimes old bedding nearby, and usually signs of wear with the grass trampled near the holes.

Difficulty: ★ ★ ★ ★ ★
Where: Old woodland and Inclosures
Date seen:

3. BANK, DITCH AND THORNS

When the tree growing Inclosures were first developed they were strongly protected by digging a deep ditch all around and throwing the soil up to make a high bank behind. A split oak fence was then built on top of the bank and a row of thorns planted just inside. The oak fences have now been replaced with wire, but around a few of the Inclosures it is still possible to see the remains of the thorn stumps inside the bank and ditch.

Difficulty: ★ ★ ★ ★ ★
Where: Inclosures
Date seen:

4. BARK STRIPPING

This is most commonly seen on small, young beech trees which are twenty to forty years old and also on a few of the limited number of sycamore trees found in the Forest. It is caused by grey squirrels as they strip the bark during May, June and July to eat the sapwood beneath. Trees seen with dead leaves during the summer are a result of this. Sometimes the trees are damaged rather than killed but even this can ruin their value.

Difficulty: ★ ★ ★ ★
Where: Inclosures and old woodlands
Date seen:

5. BEECH GARDEN

Beech gardens develop on the stumps of old beech trees which have either been blown down during winter storms or have been cut down because they are unsafe. The stumps are found throughout the old woodlands and are known as gardens because as they gradually rot they provide a home for a whole range of plants and ferns and, during the autumn, many fungi. Sometimes small holes can be seen which have been made by bank voles living under the stump.

Difficulty: ★ ★ ★
Where: Old woodland
Date seen:

6. BEECH POLLARD

Pollarding, which involves cutting off a tree at head height, was once widespread in the Forest because as the new shoots developed they were out of the reach of the ponies and deer. Much timber was produced in this way until it was made illegal in 1698. Today, a good number of ancient pollarded beech trees, all over three hundred years old and all with many branches starting some three metres above ground level, remain scattered throughout the Forest.

Difficulty: ★ ★
Where: Old woodland mainly
Date seen:

7. BOG MYRTLE

Also known as sweet gale, bog myrtle grows to a height of 60 to 120 centimetres in generally wet and boggy situations and often covers quite large areas. When the leaves are crushed they have a very distinctive sweet smell and at one time they were used to flavour beer. The plant is also reputed to repel insects and some people believe that a twig of it in the lapel or hat will keep the flies away during the summer.

Difficulty: ★ ★
Where: Wet or boggy
Date seen:

8. BRACKET FUNGUS

Often two, three or more fungi will be seen growing together on old, dead and decaying beech trees which are still standing. They are quite hard, dark coloured above and bright white beneath. Once established they continue to grow for a number of years and some of the older ones can be 50 centimetres or more across. They produce lots of very fine almost dust-like spores which are a distinctive rusty-red colour and readily spread by the wind.

Difficulty: ★ ★
Where: Old woodlands
Date seen:

9. BRUSHER MILLS

THIS STONE MARKS THE GRAVE OF
HARRY MILLS,

A hundred years ago Brusher Mills was famous as a snake-catcher and spent much of his life living in a small hut in the woods. It is thought he caught well over 30,000 snakes during his life, including a great number of the poisonous adder, many of which he sold to the Zoological Gardens in London. Today there is a public house named in his memory and his beautifully carved gravestone can be found in the local churchyard.

Difficulty: ★ ★
Where: Village
Date seen:

10. CONAN DOYLE GRAVE

Sir Arthur Conan Doyle achieved fame and success as an author and is probably best known for his Sherlock Holmes stories. He bought a holiday home at Bignell Wood near Minstead and one of his books, *The White Company*, is partly set here and in other parts of the Forest. He is buried in the local churchyard beneath a large spreading oak. The pretty church is well-known for its unusual three-decker pulpit.

Difficulty: ★ ★
Where: Village
Date seen:

11. CONTROLLED BURN

Every year some 400 to 500 hectares of heathland are burnt to destroy the old heather and gorse, which is of limited use to the stock and heathland wildlife. It is always done during the winter months when the ground is wet, so that only the tops will burn and not the roots. Many small areas are burnt to make up the total and these can be seen at various stages of regrowth, often with a good flush of grass, throughout the Forest.

Difficulty: ★ ★
Where: Heathlands
Date seen:

12. CORDWOOD

Some commoners have the right to fuelwood from the Forest. The wood is cut by the Forestry Commission into 4 feet (1.2 metres) lengths and stacked 4 feet (1.2 metres) high in long lines by the side of the Inclosure rides. These are then divided using pieces of upright branch into sections 8 feet (2.4 metres) long which are known as cords. Each cord in the Inclosures is numbered and every autumn the commoners are told where the wood is stacked and which cord number or numbers they are entitled to.

Difficulty: ★ ★ ★ ★ ★
Where: Inclosures
Date seen:

13. CREEP

These are often seen along Inclosure fences where the deer, despite being able to easily jump over them, prefer to push under. Even the old bucks with their huge antlers will squeeze through rather than jump. The creeps can be quite deep as generation after generation of deer, and sometimes other animals, use the same route. Quite often crotties (droppings) and slots (hoof prints) will be found nearby.

Difficulty: ★ ★ ★ ★
Where: Inclosures
Date seen:

14. CROTTIES

Deer droppings are often known as crotties or fewmets and, like other signs, are a good indication that deer live in an area. They are always black and glossy when fresh. The deer feed and are active during the early mornings and evenings and it is quite common to see crotties on lawns which are popular with people during the day. You are unlikely to see deer as well, as they will probably be resting in a nearby wood.

Difficulty: ★ ★ ★ ★ ★
Where: General
Date seen:

15. DEER FENCE

The deer fences, some two metres high, can be seen round some of the Inclosures also around areas of newly planted trees. Although ordinary strand wire fences are good enough to keep out the ponies, deer will readily jump over or push under them to get at the succulent young trees. So it is well worth the additional cost of the high fences to save the valuable saplings from damage.

Difficulty: ★ ★ ★ ★
Where: Inclosures
Date seen:

16. DEER REFLECTORS

The deer reflectors seen by the side of some of the busy roads are designed to reflect the light from car headlights into the woods to frighten the deer away from the roadside. Although they do help in especially dangerous areas, some 80 to 90 are still killed on the roads each year. This is often because people do not realise that when one deer dashes across the road it is invariably followed by others.

Difficulty: ★ ★
Where: Roadside
Date seen:

17. DEER SLOTS

Deer tracks are usually known as slots. They are often seen along muddy paths in woodlands and elsewhere as the deer move between their feeding and resting areas. In the photograph the slots through the centre were made when the ground was very soft after rain and later, when the ground was drier and harder, more deer passed to the right leaving much shallower marks. All are much smaller than the large semi-circular print left by a pony.

Difficulty: ★ ★ ★ ★ ★
Where: General
Date seen:

18. DO NOT FEED THE PONIES

When a pony sees or smells food it will often wander across hoping for a titbit. Sadly some people are silly and give them food, and as this happens over the weeks they gradually change from hoping to expecting and then finally demanding to be fed. At this stage many of them will readily kick and bite if they are not given food and this often causes injuries. Can you find one of the original signs warning people?

Difficulty: ★ ★ ★
Where: Car parks, roads.
Date seen:

19. DONKEYS

The commoners who have the right to graze ponies and cattle are also allowed to turn out donkeys to feed on the Forest. Every year some seventy to eighty can be seen with many of them preferring to live in and around the villages, such as Beaulieu, Brockenhurst and Burley. Some make part of their living trying to beg for food and searching the litter bins, others by feeding along the grassy verges and hedgerows.

Difficulty: ★ ★ ★
Where: Near villages
Date seen:

20. DOUGLAS FIR

The tree is native to western North America and was introduced to this country by David Douglas in 1827. In addition to being widely grown as a timber crop, there are many huge specimen trees planted in the 1860's in the Forest, especially along the Ornamental Drive to the west of Brockenhurst. The cones which are often found beneath the trees have very distinctive three-pronged papery bracts showing from beneath each scale, whilst the needles have a characteristic citrus smell when crushed.

Difficulty: ★
Where: Inclosures
Date seen:

In addition to the many streams meandering through the Forest, there are also a good number of drainage ditches which were dug in the past to drain the land and hopefully improve the grazing for the stock. Although they cannot be seen, many lawns also have a network of underground pipes to help the drainage. The ditches vary in size but can always be told from streams by being very straight.

Difficulty: ★ ★
Where: Lawns and some heaths
Date seen:

22. FIREWOOD TREE

Wood burning is still common in the Forest and a number of commoners have the right to fuelwood for burning at home. In some of the old woodlands it is also possible to buy fallen trees to use as firewood. Usually the local keeper will meet the purchaser at the tree, when a price will be agreed and the tree sprayed to indicate that it has been sold. It then has to be moved by the end of the following month.

Difficulty: ★ ★ ★ ★
Where: Old woodlands
Date seen:

23. FRAYED PINE

On the open heathland where self-sown Scots pine trees are frequently seen, a number of small trees often show signs of damage. Sometimes the bark is rubbed away, sometimes small branches broken off. The damage is caused by deer – usually red deer on the open heath – fraying the trees with their antlers as a way of marking their rutting territory. This usually happens during October with the damage being a metre or so above the ground.

Difficulty: ★ ★ ★ ★ ★
Where: Heathland
Date seen:

24. FUSED TREES

Where two trees of different species grow so closely together that they actually blend like Siamese twins, it is known as inosculation. Often it occurs with oak and beech, two of the more common trees, as in the photograph, but it can also happen to other species as well. Sometimes fusing occurs when two trees of the same species blend together or perhaps some of their branches join as one. Although fairly common, both can be difficult to spot.

Difficulty: ★ ★ ★ ★
Where: Woodlands
Date seen:

25. HEDGED GORSE

The winter months can be difficult for the ponies and donkeys. Some live in woodland areas where they find plenty of shelter from the bad weather and generally lots of holly for food. But those living on the heaths rely on the gorse. The large areas of gorse, known as gorse breaks, provide both shelter and food. In some cases the gorse is eaten so regularly that the bushes take on a smooth appearance, almost like a well-clipped hedge.

Difficulty: ★ ★ ★
Where: Heathlands
Date seen:

26. HEDGED HOLLY

Scattered among the trees in some of the woodlands, areas of very low holly will be found which are barely half a metre high. These are not young, small bushes but holly that has been so constantly browsed since it was young that the trees have never been allowed to develop. This is mainly caused by the ponies and sometimes the deer. It is a mystery why this should happen to some holly when other trees nearby are left almost untouched.

Difficulty: ★ ★ ★ ★
Where: Woodlands
Date seen:

27. HIGH SEAT

Because deer have no natural predators and their numbers increase each year following the birth of the young, a number have to be culled to avoid them either causing damage or starving during the winter due to lack of food. The culling is done by the keepers, who are skilled marksmen, using rifles from the high seats which are found throughout the Forest. Being high, the deer can neither see nor scent the keepers, who normally work very early in the morning when it is quiet.

Difficulty:　★ ★ ★
Where:　　　Most areas
Date seen:

28. HIGHLAND CATTLE

Cattle numbers vary from year to year but at the moment there are some 3000 to be seen feeding on the open Forest with all of them, like the ponies, being owned by the commoners. There are many different breeds including these very distinctive highland cattle with their long shaggy coats and imposing horns. Although they look fierce, they are quite gentle, as no animal is allowed on the Forest which might be a danger to the public.

Difficulty: ★ ★ ★
Where: Lawns and heathland
Date seen:

29. HOLLY POLLARD

Throughout the old woodlands small areas will be seen where the holly trees have been cut off at head height. This is known as pollarding and is done during the winter when the cut branches provide valuable additional food for the ponies. After pollarding the holly quickly starts to regrow, and with so much of it in the Forest there is sufficient for some to be cut every year to provide extra food.

Difficulty: ★ ★ ★
Where: Old woodlands
Date seen:

30. HORSE RIDERS

Horse riding is very popular in the Forest because there is so much open ground. Many local people own a pony and with the various stables in the area and people bring-ing ponies in for a day's riding, there is some concern about erosion, which is partly caused by the riders. This is because, unlike the commoners' ponies which roam the Forests, riding horses all have metal shoes that can cut up the ground, especially when it is wet.

Difficulty: ★ ★
Where: General
Date seen:

31. HUMMOCKS

These are not often seen outside the Forest and are sometimes mistaken for ant hills. They are caused when wet
ground is drained by ditches to improve the grazing for
the ponies and cattle. As the level of the water falls and
the ground slowly dries and shrinks, the many clumps of
tussock grass which grow in damper areas gradually die off.
It is these clumps of old grasses that gradually harden to
form the hummocks.

Difficulty: ★ ★ ★ ★
Where: Lawns
Date seen:

32. INCLOSURE NAME PLATE

There are about one hundred named Inclosures in the Forest where the commercial timber is grown, with the majority being first planted between 1700 and 1870. In recent times all were provided with plates on the Inclosure gates showing the name and date of first Inclosure. As the gates are gradually replaced because of age or damage, the name plates are not being renewed, but a good number of them can still be found.

Difficulty: ★ ★ ★ ★ ★
Where: Inclosures
Date seen:

33. KEEPERS' VEHICLE

There are twelve keepers employed by the Forestry Commission to look after the Forest, each with his own particular area. Their work is very varied and includes monitoring the wildlife such as badgers, foxes and butterflies together with any rare species that occur, as well as controlling deer and squirrel numbers and ensuring that the bye-laws are upheld. Their specially designed vehicles are large enough to carry all their equipment and dogs, and are often seen around the Forest.

Difficulty: ★ ★ ★
Where: Roads
Date seen:

34. KNIGHTWOOD OAK

In the past it was common to give names to especially big or unusual trees. Most of these have now gone, but one of the biggest and best remaining is the Knightwood Oak. It is a pollarded tree some 400 to 500 years old and is still growing. In 1863 its girth was 17 feet 4 inches (5.2 metres) and is now well over 21 feet (6.5 metres). Nearby is the Queen's Oak which was planted by the Queen when she visited in 1979 to celebrate the nine hundredth anniversary of the Forest.

Difficulty: ★
Where: Near roadside
Date seen:

35. LARCH

There are three species of larch growing in the Inclosures, the European, the Japanese and a cross between the two. All of them look very similar and all are unusual for conifers in shedding all their needles each winter. They are especially pretty in the spring when the small bright coloured female flowers appear looking like miniature cones. These are closely followed by the tufts of emerald green needles which slowly get darker before turning straw-coloured in the autumn and finally falling.

Difficulty: ★ ★ ★
Where: Inclosures
Date seen:

36. LIFE BELT

There are a good number of ponds scattered throughout the Forest. Some of them are quite shallow and are just to provide a supply of water for the ponies and other stock, but others are as a result of digging gravel or marl and can be quite deep. Life belts can often be seen near the more popular ponds where people go to feed the ducks, and near the few ponds where fishing is allowed.

Difficulty:　★ ★
Where:　　Ponds
Date seen:

37. METAL INCLOSURE MARKER

When the trees were first planted the Inclosures were securely fenced to protect the trees from damage by the ponies and deer. As the tree grew sufficiently large to be safe from damage all the fences were thrown down. When the trees were eventually felled and a new crop planted the fences were put up again. In a number of Inclosures the metal markers erected about one hundred years ago explaining this background still remain and are usually found just inside the gates.

Difficulty: ★ ★ ★ ★ ★
Where: Inclosures
Date seen:

38. MILESTONE

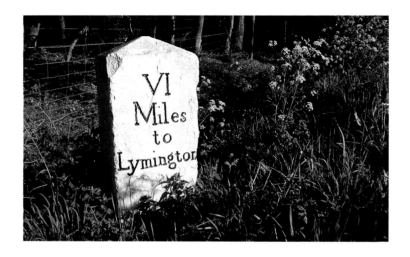

In the 18th century many of our present-day main roads were turnpikes, where the people using them had to pay a toll which was then used to maintain the road. The Turnpike Trusts that looked after them often used a distinctive design of milestone for their own particular road. The triangular one shown in the photograph was used on the Lymington-Lyndhurst-Totton road from 1765. Other designs can still be seen today along the A31 and A35 roads in the Forest.

Difficulty: ★ ★ ★
Where: Roadsides
Date seen:

39. MOUNTAIN BIKES

Cycling is a fast growing pastime in the Forest and as well as people bringing their own bikes, they can also be hired from various centres such as Brockenhurst and Burley. Cycling is allowed on the gravel tracks and a few other areas but not over the open Forest. This is partly because of the disturbance to wildlife such as ground nesting birds, and partly so that some areas can be kept quiet and peaceful as much of the Forest once was.

Difficulty: ★ ★
Where: General
Date seen:

40. MOTHER TREES

After various thinnings to give the remaining trees more space to grow, the conifers in the Inclosures are finally felled when they are about sixty years old. But rather than cut all of them down it is usual in the Forest to leave a few trees scattered through the area. These are sometimes called Mother Trees, and as well as looking better than bare ground, the seed they produce results in new trees developing which is known as natural regeneration.

Difficulty:　★ ★ ★
Where:　　　Inclosures
Date seen:

41. NAKED MAN

This is all that remains of an ancient oak which was once used as a gibbet tree where criminals were hanged and their corpses left as an example to others. Although now quiet, at the time the tree was in regular use there was a quite busy road running nearby. It ran parallel to the Inclosure, across the main road, and then on towards Burley where a mile-stone can still be seen next to what now appears to be a heathland track.

Difficulty: ★
Where: Heathland
Date seen:

42. NIBBLED HOLLY TRUNK

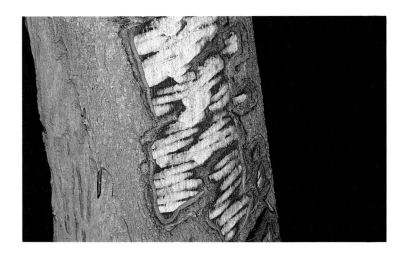

During the second part of the winter when nearly all the grass from the previous season has been eaten, the ponies have to find other foods. Both holly and gorse are eaten and, surprisingly, they often nibble the bark of the holly trees. When the bark has been freshly eaten the teeth marks can easily be seen, but after a few years it just leaves a scar. Sometimes so much is eaten that the tree eventually dies.

Difficulty: ★ ★ ★
Where: Old woodlands
Date seen:

43. NUTHATCH NEST

Nuthatch are coloured bluish-grey above with pale chestnut-coloured flanks and are found throughout the year living in old woodlands. Much of their life is spent searching for food on trunks and branches, and they are our only bird which can walk both down as well as up a tree trunk. They nest in tree holes and use mud, which sets as hard as concrete, to reduce the hole to nuthatch size, making it very secure and readily recognisable.

Difficulty: ★ ★ ★ ★ ★
Where: Old woodlands
Date seen:

44. PICNIC TABLE

Every year some nine million people visit the Forest, some coming to stay on holiday and others to enjoy a day out from the surrounding areas. Unlike some country parks, there are few facilities provided for the visitors. This helps to protect the area from becoming too commercialised and spoiling the natural scenery. However, there are a few picnic tables which are usually found near the more popular areas.

Difficulty: ★ ★
Where: Lawns and near some ponds
Date seen:

45. PIGS

The commoners turn out pigs for two months each autumn during what is known as the pannage season. The main reason is for them to eat all the fallen green acorns, because if too many are eaten by the ponies they can develop acorn poisoning and sometimes die. Pigs with sucking piglets are allowed on the Forest at any time, and in the areas near Fritham and Bramshaw they can usually be found throughout the year.

Difficulty: ★ ★ ★
Where: Usually woodlands
Date seen:

46. PONY COLLAR

Despite a 40 mph speed limit on all the unfenced roads, 150 to 160 ponies and other stock are still killed or injured by vehicles each year. Many of these accidents occur at night. On the roads crossing open areas such as heathland, the vegetation is cut back for about fifteen metres either side the road so the animals are more noticeable. And now many of the ponies are being fitted with reflective collars to try and make them even more visible after dark.

Difficulty: ★ ★
Where: General
Date seen:

47. PONY POUND

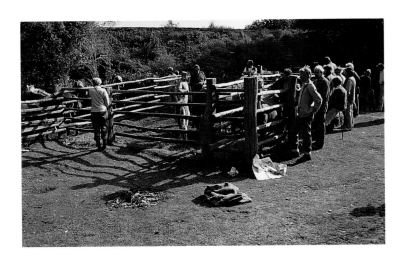

The small wooden pounds can be found in various parts of the Forest where they are usually used only once a year during the annual drift or round up. Between mid-August and early November all the ponies are rounded up in turn from some three dozen parts of the Forest ready for marking. The drifts are organised by the agisters who are paid by the commoners to supervise their stock, and they are assisted by other riders.

Difficulty: ★ ★ ★ ★
Where: General
Date seen:

48. PONY SALES

Although this complex of animal pens is usually seen empty, it is where the New Forest pony sales take place five or six times a year. They are always held on a Thursday with the first one usually in early May, the last in November, and the other three or four in between. A sale normally lasts most of the day. With as many as four to five hundred ponies changing hands and a number of stalls selling a variety of items, it is a popular day out.

Difficulty: ★
Where: Roadside
Date seen:

49. PORTUGUESE FIREPLACE

During the First World War (1914-1918) large areas of the Forest were used to help the war effort and many foreign troops were stationed here. The fireplace, which can easily be seen from the minor road nearby, is all that remains of the cook-house used by Portuguese soldiers stationed here to help produce the vast quantities of timber needed during the war. Originally the fireplace was a little further east nearer the stream.

Difficulty: ★
Where: Roadside
Date seen:

50. RIDE REPAIRS

All the Inclosures have hard gravel rides which are suitable for heavy timber lorries to use. When timber is being felled and extracted the big machines used often damage the smaller grassy rides, especially during the winter when the ground is soft. When the timber felling has finished other machines are brought in to repair this damage. The ride is then closed and a notice posted to allow time for the grass to regrow and the ride to recover.

Difficulty: ★ ★ ★ ★ ★
Where: Inclosures
Date seen:

51. ROWAN

Also known as the mountain ash, the rowan is quite small and is usually found growing as a solitary tree in the Forest. In May it is covered with a mass of white flowers which are followed by a vivid show of bright red berries in August. The berries are very attractive to blackbirds and thrushes and, being rich in vitamin C, were once used to make a drink to prevent scurvy. The tree was also believed to provide protection against witches.

Difficulty: ★ ★
Where: Old woodland, some Inclosures
Date seen:

52. RUFUS STONE

During August in the year 1100 whilst a group of the royal household was out hunting deer, an arrow shot by Sir Walter Tyrrell glanced off an oak tree and instantly killed William Rufus, King William II. Whether it was an accident or the murder of a hated King, nobody knows. The original stone memorial was erected some hundreds of years after the event but eventually became so damaged by visitors that it was encased in the present iron memorial in 1841.

Difficulty: ★
Where: Roadside
Date seen:

53. SHADING

During the hot days of summer the ponies often gather together in groups on the roads, on the heaths, or sometimes under trees in areas known as shades to stand out the heat of the day. In the evening, as the temperature falls, they all wander off to spend the night feeding, only to gather again the following day if the hot spell continues. When shading they often stand head to tail to keep the flies away from each other with their flicking tails.

Difficulty: ★ ★
Where: General
Date seen:

54. SHETLAND PONY

In addition to the 3000 or so New Forest ponies turned out each year, there are also a number of Shetland ponies. They can be seen in various colours with all of them being small and standing less than 10 hands (91cm) high. Compared to the New Forest ponies they generally look quite tubby with a long mane and tail and, in winter, a long thick coat as well. They are seen in various parts of the Forest, especially around Stoney Cross and Brockenhurst.

Difficulty: ★ ★
Where: Usually heaths and lawns
Date seen:

55. SIKA MARKS

Although not a native species, sika deer are now well established in this country. In the Forest they arrived some ninety years ago and there is now a group of about a hundred which live mainly in the Frame Heath Inclosure area. During the rutting or mating period when the stag gathers a group of hinds, he often marks his territory with his antlers, leaving deep score marks about a metre above the ground on the larger tree trunks.

Difficulty: ★ ★ ★ ★ ★
Where: Inclosure
Date seen:

56. SKEWBALD PONY

There is no limit to the breed of pony that can be depastured or grazed on the Forest, but with the exception of a number of Shetland ponies the great majority are the true New Forest breed, which should not be more than 14.2 hands high (147cm). The most common colour is bay (chestnut-brown) with all other colours being accepted except skewbald (brown and white) and piebald (black and white). But a few of these can still be seen on the Forest.

Difficulty: ★ ★ ★
Where: Heaths and lawns
Date seen:

57. SQUIRREL TABLE

Grey squirrels eat a wide range of foods with pine cones, mainly Scots pine, being a particular favourite. Sometimes the cones are eaten in the tree and the remains dropped to the ground below, but often they are taken to a flat tree stump where the scales are removed to get at the seeds below. Usually all that is left is the bare stem of the cones and a good scattering of bitten off scales all around.

Difficulty: ★ ★ ★ ★ ★
Where: Inclosures and old woods
Date seen:

58. SPARROWHAWK KILL

Sparrowhawks are now becoming quite common following a long period when their numbers were very low due to chemical poisoning. With broad, rounded wings they are able to fly at great speed through the woodlands to catch their prey of smaller birds. Although they can be difficult to see, the scattering of feathers on the woodland floor is where a kill has been made before the prey is taken to a favourite plucking post to be eaten.

Difficulty: ★ ★ ★ ★ ★
Where: Old woods and Inclosures
Date seen:

59. STILE

All three main roads running through the Forest are now fully fenced. This is intended to stop the stock wandering onto the roads rather than to stop people going into the Forest. Similarly, all the gates leading onto these roads are padlocked to avoid them being left open accidently. At the time of fencing numerous stiles were provided to give people access and although many have now gone, a good number still remain.

Difficulty: ★★
Where: Roadsides
Date seen:

60. STOCK ROAD SIGN

ANIMAL DEATHS

High Risk Road for 7 miles

A huge number of ponies, cattle, donkeys and pigs have been killed and injured on the Forest roads since the very first pony was killed by a car in 1903. And accidents still continue. Many ideas have been tried to reduce the accident rate, including fencing all the main roads and, more recently, introducing a 40mph speed limit on all the roads which have not been fenced. Various road signs have also been used, including this one which can still be seen by the side of some roads.

Difficulty: ★ ★
Where: Roadsides
Date seen:

61. SWEET CHESTNUT

This tree is sometimes known as the Spanish chestnut and was originally introduced to Britain almost 2000 years ago by the Romans. The leaves are long and narrow with saw-tooth edges whilst the bark on the trunks of the older trees usually spirals. It is planted in a number of the Forest Inclosures and the timber is used for a variety of purposes. The chestnuts in their prickly covers are popular in the autumn with both people and animals.

Difficulty: ★ ★
Where: Inclosures
Date seen:

62. TAIL MARK

When the ponies are rounded up each year they are all taken to one of the pounds to be marked. The young ponies are branded to show who owns them and the older animals are tail marked to indicate that they have been rounded up and recorded. The tail marking involves cutting the hair of the tail to one of four different shapes depending upon which quarter of the Forest the pony normally lives.

Difficulty:　★ ★
Where:　General
Date seen:

63. THATCH WITH BIRD

Although nearly all the old cob-built (a type of clay mixed with straw or heather) cottages have now gone a good number of thatched properties can still be seen around the Forest villages, most of which are thatched with straw. Some are quite distinctive in having a small thatched peacock on the roof. Sometimes there are two peacocks together and sometimes one at either end of the roof, usually indicating the work of Simon Sinkinson, a local thatcher.

Difficulty: ★ ★ ★ ★
Where: Villages
Date seen:

64. TIMBER STACK

The Inclosures were originally used to grow oak trees for use by the Royal Navy to build wooden warships, but today almost 70% are used to grow conifers which develop much more quickly. The individual Inclosures are only worked one year in five to limit disturbance, especially to the wildlife. Even so, each year some 38,000 cubic metres or about 2,000 lorry loads of timber are produced. The timber stacks at the ride-side often have initials sprayed on them to indicate which timber merchant has bought the wood.

Difficulty: ★★
Where: Inclosures
Date seen:

65. TREE SHELTERS

These plastic tubes, which are a metre to a metre and a half high, are sometimes known as Tuley Tubes after the name of the Forestry Commission employee who first developed the idea. In the Forest they are used whenever a broadleaf or hardwood tree, like beech or oak, is planted. The tubes protect the newly planted trees from damage by animals and because they act like a miniature greenhouse, they allow the tree to develop very quickly.

Difficulty: ★ ★ ★
Where: Inclosures
Date seen:

66. THE TRUSTY SERVANT

This unusually named public house, which is in the middle of a small village overlooking the tiny green where ponies often graze and with the village church nearby, takes its name from a picture hanging in Winchester College. It describes what was considered to be the perfect servant some three hundred years ago and uses animals to illustrate the ideal such as an ass for patience, a stag for speed and a pig which will eat practically anything!

Difficulty: ★
Where: Village
Date seen:

67. TUNNEL SPIDER

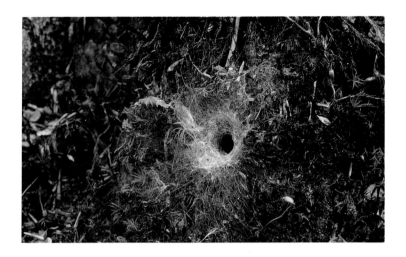

Often seen on heathlands, the spider builds a web level with the ground. This is sometimes 30 centimetres or more across and in the middle there is a tunnel about 1 centimetre across and 10 centimetres deep where the spider waits patiently for its prey. When an insect gets caught on the web the spider rushes out and takes it to the bottom of the tunnel where it is eaten or sometimes wrapped in silk and stored in the spider's larder for later.

Difficulty: ★ ★ ★ ★ ★
Where: Heathland
Date seen:

68. UNDERPASS

There are a number of underpasses or creeps passing beneath the main roads in the Forest. These were built, at some considerable expense, when the three main roads were finally fenced to keep the stock off them in the 1960's and 1970's. Although often rather wet and muddy for people to use, especially during the winter, without them the ponies would not be able to wander freely throughout the Forest as they are entitled.

Difficulty: ★ ★
Where: Roads
Date seen:

69. WATER TROUGH

All the ponies live in groups in their own part of the Forest known as their haunt. To survive they need a good area of grazing, shelter and a supply of water. This means that they cannot use some parts of the Forest at all because one of their requirements is missing. In the past lawns have been made and ponds developed and in some areas water troughs built all so the stock can make greater use of the Forest.

Difficulty:　★ ★ ★ ★
Where:　Heathland, some lawns
Date seen:

70. WAYMARK POST

There are waymarked walks of various distances in different parts of the Forest, some through Inclosures and old woodlands and others following the course of streams. The wooden posts with different coloured rings show the route, which invariably has a hard track suitable for the disabled. A leaflet is available at the start of most walks describing the route, and they make a good introduction to the Forest for those who do not wish to explore for themselves.

Difficulty: ★
Where: Various
Date seen:

71. WOOD ANT NEST

The wood ant is our largest ant species and is usually welcomed by foresters because of the great number of harmful insects it kills in woodland during the summer. The sometimes huge nests, which often persist for years, are usually found along the sunny rides and edges of conifer Inclosures. Stopping too long by a nest is not advised as the ants have the ability to spit formic acid which feels very similar to nettle stings.

Difficulty: ★ ★ ★ ★
Where: Inclosures mainly
Date seen:

72. WOODEN LITTER BINS

These can be found in many of the car parks and all of the busy areas where the wooden design of the bins is intended to make them blend with the Forest surroundings. In the summer months they usually need to be emptied at least once a day and every year well over 150 tons of rubbish is collected from them. In the quiet of the early morning it is common to see both grey squirrels and jackdaws venturing inside the bins looking for scraps of food.

Difficulty: ★
Where: Most areas
Date seen:

USE THE VOUCHER FOR FREE
CHILD ENTRY TO THE

NEW FOREST
MUSEUM & VISITOR CENTRE
LYNDHURST, HAMPSHIRE

You won't really discover the New Forest until you visit the New Forest Museum & Visitor Centre, which is open all the year round from 10 am and is situated in the main car park in Lyndhurst, the capital of the New Forest (Tel: 01703 283914).

There is no other place that tells the story of the New Forest, its history, traditions, character and wildlife. Enjoy 'The Changing Forest' picture show, come face to face with the Forest characters – like Brusher Mills the snake catcher and Alice in Wonderland. Uncover the 'Feely Log' and reveal the wildlife secrets in our Forest hide. Test your knowledge on our Computer Data Banks and complete the children quiz challenge!

All the secrets of the Forest under one roof

VOUCHER
'Child Goes Free'

Present this voucher when you pay for admission and one child (4-14 years) will be admitted free to the New Forest Museum when accompanied by a full-paying adult.

(Not valid in conjunction with any other offer)